Flour, Water, Salt

RUTH BAVETTA

FUTURECYCLE PRESS

www.futurecycle.org

Library of Congress Control Number: 2016942598

Published by FutureCycle Press
Lexington, Kentucky, USA

ISBN 978-1-942371-04-5

For Leif
who has cheered me on for 43 years

CONTENTS

Flour

Water

Salt

Flour

MATINS

Bread begins with the field,
with the grain bending its head
before the drifts and cracks
of wind and rain. It begins
with the yeast, blooming
in water warm as our bodies,
sugar, sweet as August heat.
Hands mixing flour,
water, salt, turning
the tendons of gluten
until they bend
to the will of the yeast.
Bake in the sun of the oven,
fill the house with praise.

THE STAFF OF LIFE

After my father retired
from teaching biochemistry and nutrition,
explaining vitamins, minerals, proteins,
and the Krebs cycle, when he ended his decades
of research on collagen, tryptophan and lysine,

he learned to make bread.
He used yeast and whole-wheat flour,
bananas, wheat germ, oats. Sometimes
cottage cheese, applesauce, raisins,
almonds, sunflower seeds, dates.

In the summer when we went to the family cabin
in the mountains by the Feather River,
we sat around the cherrywood table in the clear light
of morning and ate Daddy's bread,
thick and rough and toasted.

CREDO

I believe in fog drifting silently
from the Pacific Ocean,
in reading until my eyes burn.
I believe in the eyes of dogs, in wild rabbits,
in Beethoven's violin concerto,
in Joshua trees that stretch their arms
against a desert dawn.
I believe in not believing
in myth, nor in wishful thinking,
nor in a supernatural figure
who stirs things from above.
I believe in the smell of fresh-cut ginger,
sun-baked kelp, orange blossoms
in hot August moonlight,
and in the grace of dinner
beautifully prepared.

IN PRAISE OF CINNAMON BREAD

Sliced and toasted, slathered
with cool yellow butter,
it wakes us to the morning
of possibility. Icing frosts
the top like the Sierra Nevada
in January. Inside, a swirl
of speckled brown spice,
the whirl of a galaxy
not yet encountered,
sprinkled with raisins
like a church of stars.

IF I WERE A MAKER OF MARZIPAN

I would propose love letters
be made only of marzipan roses,
lullabies of sweet marzipan apples,
invitations of marzipan oranges glowing
in the light of pleasant expectations.
Almonds to snare the sun, sugar
to sweeten the soul. The honeyed heart
of a fruity stollen, the pale green
shroud covering the indulgence
of a Swedish princess cake. The apples,
bananas, pears, and pineapples of Sicily's
frutta Marturana. Aphrodisiac
of one night and a thousand. Taste.
If this isn't love, what is?

GRANDMOTHER'S BIRD'S NEST PIE

Apples from a new autumn—
peel, slice, nestle their curves in the pan.
Her hair went white. Mix flour
from the green canister, sugar
from the blue. She got old and died.
Add buttermilk, thick as love,
baking powder, egg. Mix until your arm
feels like her slumping shoulders.
Pour batter over apples. While it bakes,
listen for her singing, "Now the day is over,"
while she stands at the sink.
Turn the pie upside down on a plate,
sprinkle with cinnamon, nutmeg,
sugar sweet as school days.
While it cools, open your recipe box,
shut her away.

QUEEN OF PUDDINGS

Over the translucent blue flame, seethe
the milk until it bubbles.

Butter melted at the thought of your hands,
sugar to sweeten the mind.

Mix in the warm press
of toasted crumbs, wet them

with the milk, add the egg of need,
lightly beaten. In the oven, heat into desire.

Spread with the wild berry
jelly of imaginings, heighten

with whites whipped
into a meringue of longing.

THE JOY OF COOKING

Tear down the walls
of your kitchen,
wear your apron tied tight
to hide the condiments of rapture.
Capture the wide face of the moon
in your largest pot. Gather
the recollection of sunlight
upon the shoulders of young women.
There is no death when our teeth
crunch chicken bones, when our tongues
are slicked with yellow fat.
There is no death
when we lick our sticky lips.
There is love in milk
and salvation in the butter of heaven.

RECIPE

Dust your thighs
with flour, shake
off the excess.
Using your bare
hands, slip
them softly
into warming
fat. Turn them
as they heat.
When they are done,
lay them down
to cool. Comb
your hair.

FEAST

You are the papaya of my life,
sweet and juicy as August heat.
You are not cool as the salmon
splayed on a plate in the back
of the refrigerator, nor sour
as the lemon in its bright
untruthful skin. You are warm
and sweet, smooth as custard
scented with vanilla. Come
into my kitchen, love,
find the feather bed of good cooking.
Let me be the stocking
on your rolling pin, the slotted spoon
of longing. Together we will find
the measuring cup of desire.

ODE TO THE TOOTHPICK

Not really tan, more like ecru,
fawn, tawny beige, presented
unshellacked and oddly

mismatched in a lidded box.
Shavings of thin veneer stamped
in clean, tapered Bauhaus lines.

Singly they have no aroma,
but place your nose
to the small blue cardboard casket

and breathe the birch woods of Maine,
white-skinned, under a sky
of Botticelli blue.

AMULETS

I buy oranges, tart and sweet,
skin thick enough
to ward off heartbreak, hives,
and winter colds. Baskets
of bananas, yellow crescents
to remind me it is always warm
somewhere. Long, sturdy streaks of carrots
like flaming swords to ward off
dragons of despair. Blushing red,
crisp and sour, apples piled
like cobblestones to throw
against the loss of love.
A parsley boa, pearls of garlic,
a pale and monstrous cauliflower
to save me from myself.

MORE THAN THIRTEEN LEMONS IN THE RAIN

The tree, not in an orchard
but alone in an overgrown garden.

The fruit, brilliant
on this grey day, each one its own sun.

Lemon after lemon after lemon,
all the same, yet none the same.

Sour surrounded by bitterness
surrounded by light.

He thought it was a ball until
the fragrance stained his fingers.

Dandelion wine and lemonade stands
and a little boy I knew before I was born.

Cadmium Yellow, Cobalt Yellow,
Mars Yellow, Hansa Yellow, Naples Yellow, Azo.

Stab a lemon with a stick of candy.
Suck the sour with the sweet.

Blood running down my mother's arms,
the lemon's thorns.

Each leaf hunches its pale shoulders
against the rain. The bark weeps.

One lemon alone at the crown,
nearest the light.

   after Wallace Stevens

PERSIMMONS

What's to say?
It's hard to write a poem
about a fruit that's Day-glo orange
with sleek and slimy flesh
like summer gone rotten.
Persnickety I am about their late
appearance on the stage,
when fall has pushed summer
to the wings, about their texture
of slugs, of blight, of a sickness
that shortens the days of August,
transforms them
into winter rain.

I AM AN APPLE ON THE WINDOWSILL

I am orange blossoms in an August night,
printer's ink under the fingernails,
Cadmium Red and Cobalt Violet,
a field of wild mustard,
dark brown faded to white.

I am the palm frond sweeping the roof,
the coyote in the canyon,
a September fire,
unread pages in a borrowed book,
the silence between the waves.

I stand near the end of my years.
I stand without the aid of gods.
I sing when I can and cry when I can't.
I am a candle burned to evening.

HERE BYGYNNETH THE TALE

I am *Little Women*
and animal crackers, *Ramona*
with oatmeal cookies, *A Tale
of Two Cities,* Oreos and milk.

The years hiss by
and there is only me, locked
into *Silas Marner,*
cheddar and kosher half-dills,
The Yellow Wallpaper
and a glass of cold buttermilk.

Formulas for Painters
explains nothing
without popcorn. *Main Street*
becomes the symbiosis
of word and food.

*If on a Winter's Night
a Traveler* found me writing
this letter to you,
there would be apples
and pears and *Art
Through the Ages.*

HONEYMOON

A rare steak in a Chinese restaurant
in Mexico City. What
got into me? The *tamales,*
the *camarones a la Veracruzana,*

the *chilaquiles* with sour cream,
the *enchiladas verdes*
marking the hours of our trip
were not enough? Sick all night,

I lay in bed on the fifth floor
of the Gran Hotel. From the Zocolo,
only the random honk or swish of tires.
Finally he stirred and woke,

whispered to me of love, of his Norway,
of snow under the streetlights, of *fiskesuppe,*
of lamb and cabbage stew keeping comfort
in place on cold winter nights,

of the simmer of the two of us
starting our lives over,
dredged in the flour of expectation,
marinated in hope.

EVIDENCE

Knife covered in peanut butter
left lying on the counter. Cheese
growing translucent in its package.
Whole wheat bread naked,
already turning to lumber
on the cutting board.
He's in his favorite chair
by the window, crumbs
on the floor, empty plate
and glass on the low bookcase.
When I come in, he turns
and says, "I love you."

GJETOST

Every morning he slices bread,
takes the cube of golden-brown
goat cheese from the refrigerator.
It tastes of thin summer rains
over Oslo Fjord, snow glittering
at the foot of the stairs,
the briny smell of the sea, sailboats
in the midnight sun, the sound
of the *trikk* pulling into the station.

SUSTENANCE

I take the roast out of the refrigerator.
It's a small one, all we need,
now that the children are grown.
I lay a couple of cloves of garlic
on the cutting board
and hit them hard with the flat of my knife.
The papery skin pops off
and the cloves crack open.

I go out into the garden
and cut a handful of Italian parsley,
make slits in the roast,
stuff them with garlic and parsley,
rub the roast with olive oil,
roll it in cracked pepper.

I put the roast on the barbecue
along with a few red potatoes
rubbed with olive oil. I lower the lid
and go into the house to make the salad.
My husband comes to set the table.
While we wait for the roast to cook,
we sit at either end of the couch, reading.

When it's time,
I put the roast and potatoes
on the old blue and white platter.
My husband opens a bottle of Chianti.
I toss the salad, he lights the candles.
We sit across from each other and eat.
Under the table,
my bare feet rest on top of his.

AUBADE WITH FRENCH TOAST

Fog obscures the house across
the street, blurs the eucalyptus
towering above the church,
smudges the blues of the ocean.
A scattering of crows swims mute
through thickened air. I've opened

the bag of bread and it's gone stale.
What's left but to make French toast?
Milk cooler than the sky, eggs
beaten creamy and pale.
Hardened bread soaked
to a second life. A pan with butter.

Air and fog sift together
like flour and water
in this wakening world.
Mornings are best taken on faith.
Don't ask for more.

LATE SEPTEMBER

and still so much to do—
the bending over the bowl
of dough, the mending
of socks worn through the toe,
the paring of peaches, lovely
in their waning.

Statice beyond the glass, lusterless,
like fog against a window, fading
purple blossoms dry
as paper. Dusk is brittle
on my shoulders. I will leave
as I came in, already falling.

Water

THE CHILDREN'S AQUARIUM

In the morning light
great shining fish
swim in the concrete tanks
of the Bergen Fish Market.
The harbor is nearby
but the children watch the tanks.
"It's like an aquarium," they say.

"Shall we have shrimp for lunch?"
we ask, "Oh, yes," answer the children.
We return with two kilos of boiled shrimp,
fresh from the North Sea.
The children are still watching the fish
swim round and round.

Along the fjord, air and water
mist together. On a grey speckled rock
I open the package of shrimp.
They lie on the white paper
like bits of coral with jet-bead eyes.
The children stare. "Eyes?
Shrimp have eyes? Gross."

They go off to the car
and sit behind the glass
eating peanut butter and jelly.
Alone in the wet grey world,
we open a bottle
of thin, cool, white wine,
and eat two kilos of precious coral.

ODE TO SARDINES

The Northern Sea,
immaculate and immense,
drops anchor
on my kitchen counter.
Moonlight, reassembled
as layers of watered silk,
head to tail,
in a bright tin coffin.

WOMAN WASHING DISHES

After dinner, alone now, passing plates
left hand to right, tipping them under
running water, sluicing fragments
of food to the bottom of the sink,

putting away leftovers, closing
the refrigerator, holding a bowl,
two forks together, another
bowl, stacking it all in the dishwasher.

Turns the water to hot, takes the big blue pot,
then the small one, scours them,
picks up the cast-iron pan, scrubs
at charred remainders, scrapes them off,

dumps them onto the pile rinsed
from the plates, sweeps
it all toward the disposal.
Turns on the water, hard,

and the remains of the last meal
they have eaten together
whirl around the sink, then down.

after Christopher Merrill

WHAT WE DID

We went to the drive-in
and ordered bacon sandwiches,
salad with Roquefort dressing.
Rotifer, he thought it was.

We drove east on the 10 to his mother's
and ate overcooked green beans,
turkey dry as sand, mashed potatoes
with lumps. Divine divinity.

We ate spaghetti cooked as in my family.
We ate fried chicken cooked as in his.
We went to parties, ate onion dip, drank
gin. We ate hamburgers and steak.

He took to party-boat fishing.
I cooked the catch he brought home.
He slammed out the door
because he didn't like fish.

I took a course in Life
Drawing. Set up my easel
in the kitchen. Burned the beef
stew. He wouldn't look.

We ate acrimony and bitterness,
the common vetch of discord.
We slept without touching,
tasted the bitter tea of regret.

He wanted to go to church,
accept the wine and wafer.
I stayed home, ate unbuttered bread.
Drank the water of discontent.

BEER

Bitter stuff.
Never drank it in college.
Didn't drink it at the Lions Club
picnic in San Bernardino even though
there was that salty ham.

Then, one of those little cans
at a gas station in the desert.
I wasn't driving. He never
let me drive. Once
on a Saturday, alone, tired
from mowing the lawn.

Years later, after bowling,
everyone laughing, joking.
Impossible to knock on the pane
of glass separating me
from those I'd known so long.
I was leaving then, although
I didn't know it.
Bitter stuff.

HARD DREAMS

A long row of them unattended,
afire with our history.
The year we went to Senegal,
the summer we used my father's spade
to bury the dog, the throne
we built in the oak tree.
All of these just tangles
in the fringe of time.

The summer when the roses died,
wild thorns at the edge of the skies,
tangerines glowing uselessly
on a white ceramic plate,
bread leavened with the soil
of our own want.
The honey these have left us
may never be unbittered.

REMIND ME

Not merely of our house
built right below the pass,
but of the kitchen curtains I sewed,
of the walls we painted, the plain
and simple bed rescued
from your mother's old garage,
the dining room chairs that squeaked
no matter what we did. How
the oven billowed smoke
to fill the rooms with veils
of grey. Of the centipedes that
found their way to every room,
the silences between us, the dust.
The wind blew, oh, the wind blew.

LAST ANNIVERSARY

Glasses of ice water sweat
between us as we face each other
across the slick surface
of the table by the window.

Restaurant air conditioning
above our heads thrusts
the Arctic down our necks.
Across town, our garden,

planted sixteen years before on rocky
alluvial soil, is set afire
by the setting sun, embers
hot as biscuits burnt.

Oh, my once-dearest,
we were so young, the future
so distant. Recklessly
we married, lay together in the heat

of valley afternoons.
Even then, in sleep you wrapped
your arms around yourself
as if you sensed impending ice.

Through the glass,
the setting sun paints us gold
and the words we cannot speak
fracture against the cold.

THE BARTENDERS'S GUIDE TO SUMMER DRINKS

Gin and tonics must be drunk
while sitting in an ancient
director's chair, feet up
on the railing of the deck,

as the late afternoon sun
slants across the meadow
and the shadows of the pines
reach out to each other.

A child ought to call from the dike.
He's landed a crappie. The smell of smoke
and charcoal starter must drift
from a deck three cabins away.

Your parents should still be alive,
your mother talking
about where she's going fishing
in the morning, your father
cracking wise, more gin than tonic.

This is the high tide of the years of gin.
When it recedes you will be able
to sweep the broken shingles of the cabin
from your shoulders.

And after the developers
create mosquito heaven
by damming the stream, the quinine
will have kept malaria away.

PHOTOGRAPH, SUMMER 1944

That's my dad standing there by the barbecue
brandishing a rack of steaks.
Big grin, hair falling over one eye.

If you were there, you'd know
my mom was sitting by the table,
spotted apron, frizzy new perm.

I was there and I know
how she mixed the marinade
of olive oil, garlic, vinegar,

how she laid each steak in it as if
she were laying a cherished child
down for a nap.

How rarely we got steak. How
young they were then.
How unsuspecting.

COLD-PRESSED EXTRA VIRGIN

My mother says I'm lucky.
When she was sixty
her crows' feet had spread
until it looked like crows
had walked all over her face.

Your skin comes from your father's side,
she says, the Italian side.
They don't get wrinkles.
It's all that olive oil.

Look at your Aunt Rosa.
Her skin was so smooth
the mortician didn't even need to use makeup.
He did, of course, they all do—
heaven knows why.
Who wants to look like a madam
when they're dead?
Don't let them do it to me.

LOSING HER BEANS

Please not the green
beans—she loves them with onion,
tomato, a bit of bacon.
Not the garbanzos,
not the hummus, oozing
with oil and garlic.
She'll try to hang on
to the baked beans,
if they're not too sweet,
and the pintos, the Great
Northerns, the dried limas
with the remains of the Sunday
ham. *Frijoles de olla, frijoles
refritos.* Small whites with roast lamb
and rosemary. Evening
comes to the nursing home.
She stares at mashed potatoes,
meatloaf, Jell-O.

IN SICKNESS AND IN HEALTH

In warm Cream of Wheat
and spaghetti with garlic and chili.
In pastina with butter,
and ribs charred over the fire.
In the gloss of wet kitchen floors
and the sheen of cherries
perfectly ripened. I watch you slip
on the moss of memory. You thumb
through a menu of words you know
but can't find. In poached eggs
and *enchiladas poblanas*.
Your lost hair, your lost
memory, your face
a rumpled napkin.

A RECIPE FOR LOSS

The funeral begins
with the melancholy of roses cut
from the axis that connects
them to the earth. With the music
of forfeiture, the prayers
of nothing-to-be-done,
the gathering of the lost
around the table—the ham,
potato salad, baked beans,
green rings of Jell-O,
coconut cake with melancholy
built into every layer. The wife
in her black dress.

GARAGE SALE

The waffle iron she got as a wedding present
in 1951. Frayed cord, baked-on grime.
Tubes of oil paints, twisted, missing
labels. Without screwing off the cap,
who's to know Thalo Green from Cobalt Blue?
Three pink bouillon cups, four saucers.
A dainty blue eggcup, pale as an April sky,
only a tiny chip on the edge. Diamonds?
Got to be rhinestones. Old *Reader's
Digest* books, boxes of *National Geographic,
The Joy of Cooking.* Ladle,
can opener, measuring spoons.
One adult tricycle, a battered walker,
sixty-four jelly jars waiting for spring.

RAIN ON INTERSTATE 5

Far below the house, the world of wet
glistens in the kiss of the storm.
The sound of tires sweeping the black
asphalt carries clearly
to my tear-streaked window. The sun,

if I could see it, would be slipping
into the sea by now.
A large automobile bleats
a complaint. A semi growls
from one gear to another.

On the back of the stove,
the soup pot offers scents of a country
where I have never been. Ginger,
hot peppers, chicken, coconut milk.

The aroma is a memory
that stays with me although it never was.
The air is cool. The stars
burn behind the clouds.

COMING TO WINTER

I've spent this winter listening
for the tapping fingers of rain
on the skylight, the unexplained
electronic chirp that haunts
the kitchen, the gurgle
of pea soup on the back
burner. I've turned my ear
toward the windup groan
of the sphygmomanometer, the whine
of the next-door dog, ever hopeful
for the return of she who won't return,
and the sound of my husband's breath
in the night.

NOCTURNE FOR WASHING DISHES

All that is left from dinner are the scraps
of the lamb chops we both like so much.

Panbroiled in the cast iron skillet,
they tint the house with their aroma.

The bones, not even dry yet,
are under the sink in a paper bag

waiting for Wednesday's truck
to grind and groan its way

up the hill. All I can see
from the kitchen window

is a pair of crows arching across
a fading sky. I imagine

the sound of wings, soft
and cushiony, pulsing against

the evening air. Again.
Yet again.

Salt

KITCHEN WINDOW

There are three charms
in my apron pocket—
a baby tooth
from my oldest child,
my mother's Phi Beta Kappa key,
and an old stove bolt
gone to rust.
They have brought me luck
thus far.

DEAR AS SALT

on Ralph Going's painting, Double Ketchup, *1996-97*

The salt stands iconic on the counter
guardianed by blood-red double ketchups,
flooded with light flowing from the right.

Sodium chloride, a molecule of two—
each harmful alone, when bonded
together they live in harmony.

Halite, hexoctahedral, isometric, perfect
cleavage. Here are pure white cubic crystals
sparkling in a stubby glass shaker.

Sought and sold for seasoning,
medicine, taxes, ketchup, the mining of silver.
Preservative for Egypt's everlasting dead.

The Princess told her father,
"You are as dear to me as salt,"
and he, offended to be compared

to such a commonplace, threatened
to banish her from the palace—until
she served him roast bream and darioles,

mustard soup, simnel cake, Swithin cream,
pasties filled with marrow, all without salt,
tasteless as a life without love.

Salt makes it harder for things to boil
and harder, too, for them to freeze.
It prevents the yeast from overflowing.

From mines, from brines, from solar heat,
symbol of fertility, symbol of purity,
regulator of the heart.

Salt is ancient, salt is eternal.
Salt is what you offer me
every night across the table.

MICE

They seldom scurry in the light,
but at night, while we're asleep,
the kitchen is theirs. If they make a sound,
it's but a faint scratching like the memory
of a branch in the wind
caressing the window.

In the morning, a few black seeds on the floor
and one small half-eaten tangerine.
I, who have listened
for their footsteps every night,
have never heard those delicate
cadenzas picked out on the red tiles,
the almost silent crunching, the cracker
wrappers crumpled in a heap.

DINNER IS SERVED

Most women who go mad, go mad in kitchens. —*Judith Newton*

I am building evidence
in the absence of a recipe.
Pages are missing.
The knife is dull as celery.
The refrigerator holds only curdled
milk, wilted lettuce,
and three old eggs. And radishes.
I could make you a necklace
of overage radishes, dark and peppery.
I think of hotcakes on a bed of onions.
What I find is a bottle opener wed
to a cheese grater gone rusty.
I would place dinner on the empty
table—caviar with custard,
fish swimming in maple syrup,
a salad of eucalyptus leaves—
but my kitchen offers only
a burned-out mixer, a dented
set of measuring spoons, and a roasting
fork which threatens my life.

THE REAL STORY

In a kitchen where the ceiling
is extremely low, the heat
from the pan of frying chicken
almost melts the rafters.
Nuts and raisins cuddle
in the muesli. Lettuce leaves
the comfort of the refrigerator,
flaps its wings, flies around the lamp.
Cans of tuna and tomatoes
creep from the pantry to make
extended love under the table.
Wine consorts with beer
to no good end. The steam
from the boiling kettle
fills the room with a promise
false as cream. The man
who comes to eat
will break your heart.

ON THE BLOCK

The chicken runs and squawks,
but as soon as my mother picks it up,
it stills. Holding it

by its scaly yellow feet,
she lays its head on a stump.
One eye looks up at her.

She slams the hatchet down.

The head lies alone on the stump,
one golden eye wide open, staring at a sky
that grows larger and larger.

THIS IS ALL I HAVE TO SAY

The endless days, the poisonous sugar
of indolence. The grapes overripe,
the oranges hopelessly sour.
He lay on the sofa
licking peanut butter from a spoon.
The dampness, the suffocation of sunlight.
Crackers molded in the cupboard,
chocolate with a scrim of pale.
He would not leave the house.
The front door was locked.
On bad days I remember this.

WEDDING CAKE

This is about roses
of spun sugar,
wax-white lilies, clouds
of baby's breath, violets
that cast no shadows.

This is about a garden
of eggshell prayers, the planting
of seeds not always
in concert, the tyranny
of encumbrance.

The sacrament
piercing her left hand,
his left palm, the last
scene at the window, the axe
in the corner.

THE MOON'S AN EMPTY FRUIT

Pale as an onion, an orange
with the color sucked out,
a bleached and naked kiwifruit,
an apple with a pockmarked skin,
a damaged sphere that has never
contained what we've ascribed
to it, the hopes of lovers, the light
for our dark nights, a guidebook
for lost and weary travelers. Hanging
improbably above us, it threatens
to ripen, to fall to earth,
soft and rotten, a turnip
without a blush.

OSSUARY

Carpals, metacarpals, phalanges, femur,
ham bone, rib roast, barbecued wings.

Hunger for gristle, sinew, tendon,
souvenirs of soup bones sewn into your pockets.

Blade cut, brisket, arm steak, shank,
sternum, ulna, Haversian canal.

A litter of chewed knucklebones
spells your life in new letters.

Calcaneus, clavicle, ligament,
marrow bone. Your only safety

is the stranger you sleep next to.
Scapula, vertebrae, acetabulum.

WHAT IT IS

The tongue is tough and warty,
must be boiled for hours
before it is tender as shame.

Trout, however, leaps almost willingly
into the pan, one eye
to the heat, the other to the eater.

Dark Bing cherries,
paperweights of juice
to wear like earrings of delight.

Crisp as honey, the apple
needs no sugar of thrills
to complete the pastry of desire.

Honeydew like a smile
from you across the table.
I want to call you mine.

SESAME BUN

Heading north on Highway 5,
cotton, almonds, plums stretching
toward white-crowned mountains.

From behind a rise, cattle pens—reeking
black muck, acres of beasts crammed
flank by shoulder. This

is the home on the range
where the Stetsons
fatten the franchise burgers.

Seeing those animals, standing dull
in a premortuarial sludge
of mud, slime and ordure,

ought to put me off my feed.
But, hey, what's a little horror
when you've got the yen for a big one?

I'll take fries with that.

PACKING MY GRANDMOTHER'S SUITCASE

You've been dead
for more than thirty years,
and you want what?
See's chocolate? Okay,
one large box; share it
any way you want.
Your Chinese silk robe?
I'm glad. Every time I've worn it
I've thought of you. Should I put in
your rosewood crutches?
They're still here
in the corner closet. How about
an extra pair of glasses?
You no longer need them?
How nice. No, I won't forget—
four bottles of Manischewitz,
five cans of imported sardines,
three tins of English tea.
Where shall I send it?

FROM THREE TO EIGHT O'CLOCK

Under the grape arbor,
Uncle Calogero sits at the table,
looks around at all of us.
Antipasto—olives, anchovies,
salami, peppers, artichoke hearts.
Shouts to the kitchen, "Rosa, come
sit down!" Spaghetti *aglio e olio*.
Passes a hunk of Parmagiano. "Here,
grate for yourself, ziggy, ziggy."
Veal cutlets in garlicky breadcrumbs
sautéed in olive oil. "Rosa,
sit down!" Looks at my boyfriend.
"Water not wine? You gonna rust your pipes."
Tenerumi with tomatoes and basilico.
"Rosa!" Crusty, chewy bread. "Rosa sit!"
Tossed green salad. "Rosa!" Fresh fruit.
Cheesecake. Espresso.
Rosa sits down.

FENNEL

When I was a kid we called it *finocchio*
and my mom bought it at the Italian grocery
or we picked it where it grew wild
in the empty lots of Los Angeles.
Now I buy it at my local market, the one
known for its gourmet stock.
They call it "sweet anise."
I guess they think their customers
can't pronounce *finocchio*.
The other day a sweet, young thing
rang up my groceries.
"Oh," she said, swinging the soft green plumes,
the sensuous white bulb,
into a plain brown paper bag,
"sweet anus."

DUCKS

is what he used to call me
because, like most American ducks,
I grew up on Long Island,
had more than my share of body fat,
and was, according to him,
a little too much for one person,
but not quite enough for two.

A WORLD WITH NO CHICKENS

No rooster to wake us,
no eggs for breakfast.
A keepsake from the farm.
A picnic under a pine tree.

What would stay behind
to nourish us? A single lonely
barbecued thigh?
An oven with no heat.
An empty platter.

Where would be the soup
for all ills, the breast
that succors us? The flight
of crispy wings around the kitchen?
A drop of wine—not enough.

THIS EXPLAINS WHY THE CHICKEN SUIT YOU ALWAYS WEAR FOR WORK IS SO DAMN HOT

a cento from googling "damn chicken"

Cook the damn chicken cutlets woman,
don't eat 'em raw!

Motherfucker got the bone
all the way out the damn chicken.

Free dating. Singles and Personals.
Best Damn Chicken Wings ever.

Erotic is using a feather, kinky
is using the whole damn chicken.

Damn chicken pocks, I'm gonna get it.
I swear I'm gonna kill him.

I need those chicken pills
so i can wear my applebottom jeans next week.

Come, eat your dinner.

SELF SERVICE

Irish stew, mashed potatoes,
spinach, sliced tomatoes.
Steam tables, shining chrome,
servers waiting, green beans,
buttered bread, people puddling
behind, Jell-O, chocolate pudding.
Can I change my mind, exchange
the meatloaf for roast beef? Go back
to pick up pickled tongue? Return
the doll I stole from Kresge's in 1944?
Oatmeal cookies, coconut cakes,
dates, roommates, jobs, chicken, baked.
Can I slip my first husband back
among the lemons? If I return
to get creamed peas, I might
decide they're not for me.
The line behind is getting longer.
My second husband's waiting
near the angel cake. Now
the line in front is shorter
than the line behind.
I'm getting closer to the end,
to the place I'll have to pay
for everything
that's on my tray.

GOING HOME

When you come to the fork in the road,
lean down and pick it up. Turn it over
in your hands, notice if it is silver or stainless
steel. Is it well used? Tines bent? Handle
skewed? Do you recognize the pattern? Raise
your head, look down the road, take the turn
that leads to the house with lights on,
roast chicken bright with juice,
mother removing her apron.

ACKNOWLEDGMENTS

Grateful acknowledgment is made the to following publications in which certain poems in this collection first appeared, sometimes in slightly different form.

Barely South: "Packing My Grandmother's Suitcase"
Ilya's Honey: "Cold-Pressed Extra Virgin"
IthacaLit: "Wedding Cake"
Kentucky Review: "Elegy for my Mother"
Naugatuck River Review: "Last Anniversary"
Nerve Cowboy: "Fennel"
North American Review: "Ode to the Toothpick"
Pirene's Fountain Beverage Anthology: "The Bartender's Guide to Summer Drinks"
Poetry New Zealand: "Sustenance"
Rattle: "Fennel"
Red Paint Hill: "Dinner is Served," "Ducks"
Slant: "Self Service"
Spillway: "Autumn Sacrifice"
The Ledge: "Last Dinner in Mohawk"
Verse Wisconsin: "Late September"
Word Soup: "Going Home"

"Dear as Salt" appeared in *Fugitive Pigments* by Ruth Bavetta (FutureCycle Press, 2013).

"Ode to Sardines" and "Feast" appeared in *Feast: Poetry and Recipes for a Full Seating at Dinner* (Black Lawrence Press, 2015).

Cover artwork, "Dining room table with flowers, near Pittsboro" by Tom Daley; author photo by herself; cover and interior book design by Diane Kistner; Legacy Sans text and titling.

ABOUT FUTURECYCLE PRESS

FutureCycle Press is dedicated to publishing lasting English-language poetry books, chapbooks, and anthologies in both print-on-demand and Kindle ebook formats. Founded in 2007 by long-time independent editor/publishers and partners Diane Kistner and Robert S. King, the press incorporated as a nonprofit in 2012. A number of our editors are distinguished poets and writers in their own right, and we have been actively involved in the small press movement going back to the early seventies.

The FutureCycle Poetry Book Prize and honorarium is awarded annually for the best full-length volume of poetry we publish in a calendar year. Introduced in 2013, our Good Works projects are anthologies devoted to issues of universal significance, with all proceeds donated to a related worthy cause. Our Selected Poems series highlights contemporary poets with a substantial body of work to their credit; with this series we strive to resurrect work that has had limited distribution and is now out of print.

We are dedicated to giving all of the authors we publish the care their work deserves, making our catalog of titles the most diverse and distinguished it can be, and paying forward any earnings to fund more great books.

We've learned a few things about independent publishing over the years. We've also evolved a unique, resilient publishing model that allows us to focus mainly on vetting and preserving for posterity poetry collections of exceptional quality without becoming overwhelmed with bookkeeping and mailing, fund-raising activities, or taxing editorial and production "bubbles." To find out more about what we are doing, come see us at www.futurecycle.org.

THE FUTURECYCLE POETRY BOOK PRIZE

All full-length volumes of poetry published by FutureCycle Press in a given calendar year are considered for the annual FutureCycle Poetry Book Prize. This allows us to consider each submission on its own merits, outside of the context of a contest. Too, the judges see the finished book, which will have benefitted from the beautiful book design and strong editorial gloss we are famous for.

The book ranked the best in judging is announced as the prize-winner in the subsequent year. There is no fixed monetary award; instead, the winning poet receives an honorarium of 20% of the total net royalties from all poetry books and chapbooks the press sold online in the year the winning book was published. The winner is also accorded the honor of being on the panel of judges for the next year's competition; all judges receive copies of all contending books to keep for their personal library.

www.ingramcontent.com/pod-product-compliance
Lightning Source LLC
Chambersburg PA
CBHW070010100426
42741CB00012B/3185